For My Love...

Copyright © 2013

All rights reserved, including the right to reproduce this book or portions thereof in any form whatsoever.

For bulk sales, book tours, or signed copies from Savannah

Contact Crestcencia.ortiz@gmail.com

ISBN-13: 978-0615937328
ISBN-10: 0615937322

About the Author and the Muse

Crestcencia Ortiz-Barnett is a new author as well as parent. Savannah, the muse, is her bonus daughter (stepdaughter). Crestcencia wanted to create a unique bond to begin their relationship and the opportunity presented itself as the man in their lives had to fulfill his duties overseas. Bonus mom and daughter found themselves building a closer relationship. They began to lean on each other for support.

Crestcencia wanted Savannah to feel closer to her father, so they sat down and tracked his journey to all of the continents he had worked on. In the process Crestcencia took notes of their conversation and the lessons she was able to teach Savannah, and compiled them into this book.

She would like to share this valuable lesson with other children in the world, to not only prepare them educationally, but to bring them "closer" to the ones they love.

Savannah, I never envisioned the joy you would bring into my life. You are the most perfect "bonus Daughter" that I could have ever imagined.

I love you, Your Bonus Mom

To my husband Jessie, thank you for your continuous support. We appreciate your sacrifice for our country and we are grateful for the life you have provided for us. We love you, Savannah and CeCe

Darilis, you are one of the most influential people in my life. Thank you for believing in me, guiding me, and helping me along the way.

To my family and friends and all the glorious people that I have had the chance to meet while traveling the world, thank you for your support!

This book is dedicated to all of the "Military Brats" and Military parents who are also sacrificing their lives with their moms, dads and children for the greater good of our country. We salute you!

For Mr. Alvin Sims, no amount of words in any number of books would be able to express the gratitude that I have for you in my heart… you saved me, - Bird

INTRODUCTION

My name is Savannah and I am 9 years old. I am in the 4th grade and learning about continents. This word sounds like [CON-TEH-NENTS] to me. Continents are really big parts of land. There are seven continents in the world. Some look like they are joined together, and others look like they are surrounded by water. Some continents have many countries, and other continents do not.

I like learning about continents because I like to keep track of where my daddy is in the world. My daddy is in the United States Air Force and his job takes him all over the world. Sometimes I get sad because I only see him once a year for a very short time, but my daddy calls me and writes me a lot. He loves to hear about what I learn in school and I love to make him proud.

I am so happy to share what I learned about continents with you!

~Savannah

Many people believe that billions of years ago, all of the continents were one big piece of land. We call this land Pangaea. It sounds like [PAN-GEE-UH]

Over the years, they say that this land broke apart and turned into seven different parts, and we now call them Continents.

AFRICA

Africa is the second largest continent. I also learned that my ancestors were brought to North America from Africa.

An ancestor is someone in your family from a very long time ago. Like your great grandfather's great grandfather.

Africa has the longest river in the world called the Nile River, and Africa also has the largest Desert in the world called the Sahara Desert.

There are 55 recognized countries in Africa.

ANTARCTICA

Antarctica is a land that is frozen. You can find it at the bottom of the globe, where the South Pole is.

Antarctica is the highest, coldest, windiest, emptiest, and even though it is made up of mostly frozen water, it is the driest place on earth.

Daddy hasn't been to this continent yet, and I hope he never has to go. I wouldn't like him to be that cold.

ASIA

Asia is the largest continent in the world and has the highest population. It means that this continent has the most people living on it.

Asia's most famous animals are reticulated pythons, pandas, tigers, yaks, cute pandas and Indian rhinoceroses

My daddy has been stationed on this continent two times already. Both times he has been stationed in South Korea, where he is right now. My Bonus (step) mom lived there too. She was an English teacher.

They were able to travel to other places in Asia like China, Thailand, and Japan. They always send me the best presents from these places!

AUSTRALIA

Australia is the biggest island. An island is a place that is surrounded by water on all sides. It is also the smallest continent in the world and sometimes called "island continent".

Australia only has one country on its continent, it is itself, Australia.

There is a very large bird on this continent but it doesn't fly. This bird is called an emu. This is also where you will find many kangaroos!

In Australia you will see more sheep than people.

Australia is also known as "The land down under".

EUROPE

Europe is the only continent that doesn't have a desert.

Famous cities like Paris and Rome are in Europe.

My Daddy was stationed in Italy for two years. He lived in a small city called Aviano. My bonus mom also lived there with my daddy for a little while, before she moved to Korea, and she always says that even though she loved daddy before Italy, she fell in love with him there. (awwww)

One of the most fun things I learned about Europe is the Tomato festival in Spain, where people throw tomatoes at each other. It sounds like fun!

NORTH AMERICA

North America is the continent that I live on.

I live in the United States of America.

You can find countries like Canada, The United States of America and Mexico on this continent.

North America is the only continent that experiences all climates. Climate means weather.

The third longest river in the world is in North America. It is called the Mississippi River. My daddy was born and raised in Mississippi. Mississippi is a state that is located in the south eastern part of The United States of America.

North America has great places to visit like the Grand Canyon, The Washington Monument, Niagara Falls and the Statue of Liberty.

SOUTH AMERICA

Africa has the longest river, but South America has the largest (biggest) and it is called, The Amazon River.

Brazil, a country in South America, makes the most coffee in the whole world.

Soccer is the most popular sport in South America.

One of the world's largest snakes is in South America, It is called an anaconda.

Thank you for learning about continents with me, I hope you enjoyed our voyage and that you take the time to do more research on all of the amazing countries within the continents! Try finding your favorite part of the world!

-Savannah

www.ingramcontent.com/pod-product-compliance
Lightning Source LLC
Chambersburg PA
CBHW060808090426
42736CB00002B/203